Bad Girls
Need Love Too

Gary Lovisi

Copyright ©2010 Gary Lovisi

Published by

Krause Publications, a division of F+W Media, Inc.
700 East State Street • Iola, WI 54990-0001
715-445-2214 • 888-457-2873
www.krausebooks.com

To order books or other products call toll-free 1-800-258-0929
or visit us online at www.krausebooks.com or www.Shop.Collect.com

Library of Congress Control Number: 2010923672

ISBN-13: 978-1-4402-1357-1
ISBN-10: 1-4402-1357-7

Cover Design by Rachael Knier
Designed by Katrina Newby
Edited by Kristine Manty

Cover image from the book, *Lingerie Ltd.*, by Ralph Dean,
Beacon Book #B300, 1960; art by R. Gifford.

Printed in China

50 NOVEL BOOK

5062

John Nemec's

FOR ADULTS

NYMPHO
NYMPHO
NYMPHO
NYMPHO
NYMPHO
NYMPHO
NYMPHO
NYMPHO
NYMPHO

WILD FOR KICKS

Fay
was madly
in love with
just one man
but her beautiful
body was constantly
urging her to any man
who could satisfy her!
Nympho . . . nympho . . .
nympho . . . that one word
haunted Chuck as he moved
from bed to bed searching for
the most sadistic sex killer on earth!

Wild For Kicks by John Nemec; Novel Book #5062, 1961.

Good Girls Go to Heaven;

Bad Girls

Go Everywhere

This is a celebration of bad girls. The really, really bad girls mothers warn their sons to stay away from, and pray their daughters will never become.

It's a good thing not everyone thinks mother knows best— or else we wouldn't have any of these wildly wanton women to delight in. Bad girls have everything figured out. They know a woman must use every weapon at her disposal, and sex is the nuclear bomb. These classic pulp fiction hussies, sluts, and tarts have heads for business and bodies for sin. Let's face it: they want what they want when they want it.

Bad girls are red lights for lust. But deep down inside, they are also hungry for love because even bad girls need love, too. These dangerous dames will try to find love with whomever they can, whether with cheating husbands, unscrupulous bosses, rich college boys, and even other women. And if they don't find love with Mr. Right, they'll often settle for Mr. Right Now. Bad girls keep searching because they know that to climb to the top, they often have to spend a lot of time on the bottom.

These tramps and vamps excite and arouse and while their charms may be had—even if it is at a price—they are never boring; because when these girls are bad, they're even better.

Gary Lovisi
Brooklyn, New York

'WAY DOWN IN THE DEEP SOUTH...
MEET THE

cotton

60c

tramps

By
KEVIN NORTH

— A STORY OF GREED AND
LUST ON A PLANTATION...
AND THE SHOCKING IMPACT
OF SEXUAL CONFLICT

Cotton Tramps by Kevin North; Playtime Book #620, 1962. Cover art by Robert Bonfils.

AN ORIGINAL PLAYTIME EXTRA-LENGTH BONUS BOOK!

Undercover Job

by Ben Daniels

The sex-hungry women told him anything he wanted to know—as long as he kept pushing the passion button!

75c

Undercover Job by Ben Daniels; Playtime Book #652S, 1963. Cover art by Robert Bonfils.

The sex-hungry wo

He stared now at the shapely lines of
her long dancer's legs.

She was built for sex.

Every creamy, tempting inch of flesh
was designed to whet and bring
fulfillment to a man's desires.
If that man was someone she liked.
And wanted. Otherwise, Jill Fischer
could probably be a cruel
hard-eyed bitch. One of those
conniving, well-educated and
beautiful young sophisticates with the
heart of a back-alley whore.
A woman like his wife Mildred
had been.

n told him anything

The bedroom door opened and Diane strode through wearing a pair of high-heel shoes. **Blonde all over she was, and even a man with Dan's slow boiling point couldn't deny that there is a vast difference between a beautiful woman in Chinese pajamas and the same woman naked.**

When She Was Bad by William Ard; Dell First Edition #B145, 1960. Cover art by Robert McGinnis.

SHAME

March Hastings

BEACON

B198
35¢
K

THE STORY OF MARIA —
WHOSE MOTHER WAS A
PROSTITUTE! COULD SHE
ESCAPE HER HERITAGE . . .
OR WOULD HER TAINTED
BLOOD BETRAY HER INTO
A LIFE OF DEGRADATION?

Shame by March Hastings: Beacon Book #B198, 1958.

Daughter of Evil!

**So young, so pure, so wonderfully
pretty—these were the words to
describe Maria.
Yet in her own mind she was already
a bad girl.
For her mother was nothing more
or less than a common prostitute.
And Maria was sure that she had
inherited the taint.**

Temptation traps a lovely young wife thrust into a fast world of exciting men.

ABC

OFFICE HUSSY

The Loves of Alice Brandt

by John Hunter

No. 767

35¢

Office Hussy by John Hunter; Star Novels #767, 1957, digest-size paperback.

Wanton Paula Was the Passion—Prize at The End Of The Race!

HOTROD SINNERS

By DON ELLIOTT

Hotrod Sinners by Don Elliott; Bedside Book #BB-1222, 1962.

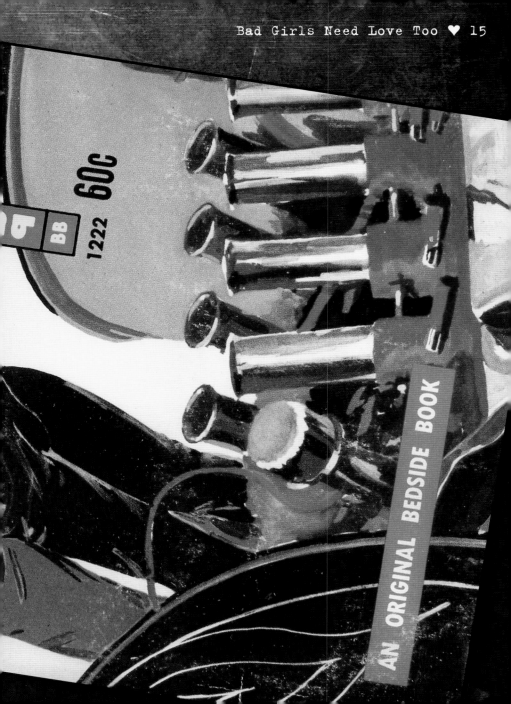

Oh, so that was the game!

She was going to claim that he
had "ruined" her—when she had
practically thrown herself on him,
and had begged him to do what
he did, and had made no bones
of her enjoyment of it!
The brass-bound gall of her!

"Are you hungry?"
"You know I am, baby."
"I mean for breakfast."
"Well, that's not what I mean."
Pat nuzzled June's shoulder, her head
swimming in the waves of
fragrant blonde curls.
"Let's—let's have breakfast later,"
June suggested, her voice suddenly
hoarse. She began undoing the
buttons of her flimsy pajamas…

THE RED SNAPPER

by BOBBY VENTS

CN 95c

INSATIABLE IN HER DESIRE FOR UNNATURAL SEX, SHE LUSTED AFTER HER BEST FRIEND'S WIFE!

The Red Snapper by Bobby Vents; All Star Books #AS55, 1965.

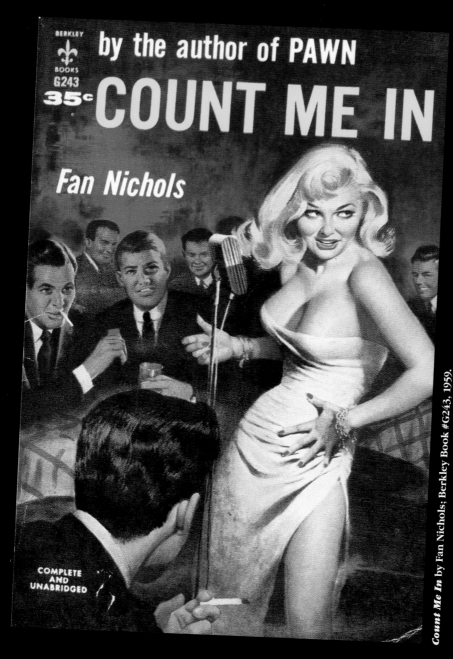

by the author of PAWN

BERKLEY BOOKS
G243
35¢

COUNT ME IN

Fan Nichols

COMPLETE
AND
UNABRIDGED

Count Me In by Fan Nichols; Berkley Book #G243, 1959.

" Gorgeous slut!

Matt Kovac was tough, but he learned the hard way that a gorgeous blond could be even tougher… Beautiful Gail Preston hated his guts. She was out to ruin him and she knew how to do it. She had her gang behind her and the whole town sewed up solid. Matt knew they would stop at nothing to keep things going her way… "

35¢
MIDWOOD

NO. 70

SIN ON WHEELS

By LOREN BEAUCHAMP
(an original novel)

THE UNCENSORED
CONFESSIONS OF A
TRAILER CAMP TRAMP

Sin on Wheels by Loren Beauchamp; Midwood Book #70, 1961. Cover art by Paul Rader.

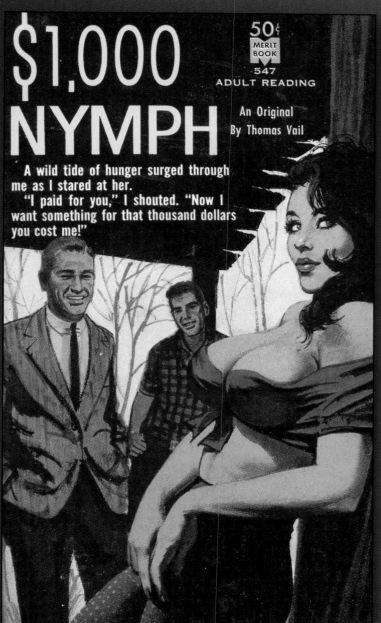

BELMONT B50-798 · 50¢

5

TUNE IN
AND
TURN ON!

VALENTINE FLYNN
NYMPHOLOGIST

Invasion of The Nymphomaniacs by Sean O'Shea; Belmont Book #B50-798, 1967.

A squeeze play in a "falsies" factory might bust it for Valentine Flynn

INVASION OF THE NYMPHOMANIACS

by SEAN O'SHEA

She put her arms around him and made him kiss her. He felt the trembling warmth in her lips and he was maddened by their greedy pressure telling him that this gorgeous co-ed wanted him. There was tight anger in his fierce convulsive embrace. "Why can't you let me alone?" he muttered. "Why can't I let you alone? We're heading for something we'd both regret, baby."

"Baby wants what she wants when she wants it."

Girl-Crazy Professor by Florence Stonebraker; Croydon Book #46, 1953, digest-size paperback. Cover art by Bernard Safran.

Psychology was his subject...co-eds his weakness

GIRL-CRAZY PROFESSOR

by Florence Stonebraker

AN ORIGINAL NOVEL

EXIT

Not a Reprint

35¢

No.46

ANC

vagabond
virgin

35c

by
J. A.
FLANNIGAN

No one had questioned her virtue . . . yet now her life depended upon it.

Vagabond Virgin by J.A. Flannigan; Newsstand Library #518, 1960. Cover art by Robert Bonfils.

Caught in the lost world of the
beatniks, Lisa's search for love leads
her to danger. Her one chance for
freedom is to prove her virginity.
Then, in a moment of passion
she destroys this one—
her only chance.
She lay beneath him crying softly.
She was no longer a virgin—
she had learned what it was like to
be taken by a man.

BEATNIK
LUST!

RUN, LEZ, RUN

95c

PEC

FL 10

By
DAVE KING

THE FINEST IN ADULT READING

Run, Lez, Run by Dave King; PEC Book #FL10, 1967.

As the other woman slowly crossed the
room toward Margo she could feel the
blood pounding in her ears,

the surge of passion
flowing over her
entire body

and a small moan of despair and
desire trembled on her lips…

She said she was ill,
that her temperature was up.
When he helped her to his bedroom,
he believed the fever bit...

This broad really was hot!

The Chinese Streetwalker by Arnold Marmor; Playtime Book #718-S, 1965.

She Had Nothing To Lose But Her Reputation

Manhandled

Whitman Chambers

First
Publication
Anywhere

Manhandled by Whitman Chambers; Monarch Books #434, 1964. Cover art by Harry Barton.

Charlie thought Sally was virginally innocent, and offered to marry her. Money-mad Eric saw her as a choice piece of merchandise, to be bought, used and resold. Cynical Mark sensed that Sally was as hip as a beatnik, and meant to prove it before his brother's very eyes.

I blushed slightly. I couldn't help it if my
breasts were as big as cantaloupes.
Everybody stared at them.

Every male wanted to touch them and squeeze them and kiss them.

It showed in their eyes.
I liked having it done, too. That was one
of my problems. That, and being too
pretty and spoiled for my own good.

95c

PEC

N-161

BLACKMAIL BITCH

BY RAY WILDE

THE FINEST IN ADULT READING

Blackmail Bitch by Ray Wilde; PEC Books #N-161, circa 1967.

30 cents

An Uptown Book

He Kissed Her

He Kissed Her There by Greg Tyler; Uptown Book #700, circa 1964.

BY GREG TYLER

She moved like all the animals of the plains effortlessly and with a grace and style that no civilized creature could have. This was only the beginning of a Wierd Wanton Affair.

K
50¢
MIDWOOD

F238

She sang for her supper,
but did something else
for her midnight snack.

The
HOT
CANARY

By JOAN ELLIS

FIRST PRINTING ANYWHERE

The Hot Canary by Joan Ellis; Midwood Book #F238, 1963. Cover art by Robert Maguire.

I was down to my garter belt now, and I wore no panties. I twisted my arms behind me to reach the hooks of my bra, thrusting my breasts forward until I saw him bite his lip.

The bra fell, then the garter belt, and I stretched with abandon.

With a cry he grabbed at me, his mouth hot on mine, his arms crushing me to him with bruising force...

Sue clung to him drunkenly.
She made no effort to ward off the
hand which caressed her. She did
not know if she was blushing
or if it was the whiskey that made
her cheeks burn. She felt full of
warmth and passion.
At that moment, she was supremely
glad that she was a woman.

Her boss believed in taking liberties!

Office Wife

RICHARD GRANT

B335
35¢
K

A CANDID
STORY OF
TWO-TIMING—
AND PLEASURE
BEFORE
BUSINESS!

Office Wife by Richard Grant; Beacon Book #B335, 1960.

A STORY OF STRANGE PASSIONS AND FORBIDDEN LUSTS THAT CHANGED A YOUNG GIRL INTO A TWISTED SINNER!

TWISTED LOVES

By Mark Ryan

bq

BB 807 aSn

50¢

THIS IS AN ORIGINAL BEDSIDE BOOK

Twisted Loves by Mark Ryan; Bedside Book #807, 1959.

Warped desires and frustrated passions turned Connie from a decent woman into a strange sinner. She learned the facts of life the wrong way by secretly observing her love-starved cousin Alice in a primitive, backwoods affair. The forbidden sight almost turned her permanently into a

twisted strumpet!

Marry for money…and love can come later—not necessarily with the same guy, was Janet's credo for happiness. Go where the rich go—do what the rich do, and make yourself available, were her methods. Janet's provocative smile and alluring body were the better mousetrap—but a mousetrap has also been known to catch a rat.

I.O.U. ME

75¢
RB106

ADULTS ONLY

THIS IS A RAM BOOK

I.O.U. Me, no author listed; Ram Book #RB106, circa 1963.

RAINBOW NO. 117

Bedroom in Hell!

AN ALCOHOLIC EX-D.A. . . . A
WOMAN OF THE STREETS . . . IN
A BEAUTIFUL FRAME OF MURDER !

A Brand
New Novel
by
NORMAN
A. DANIELS

Author of
Mistress on a
Death Bed

A RAINBOW BOOK

35¢

Curiosity had always been her main incentive toward sex. When you let sex go, let boys follow their natural instincts, it gave you things to wonder about.

But you learned fast in a motel.

Like from the guy who had enlightened her one day in his cabin at the motel. He'd asked her point blank in so many words for what he wanted, and pushed a ten dollar bill into her shirt pocket at the same time.

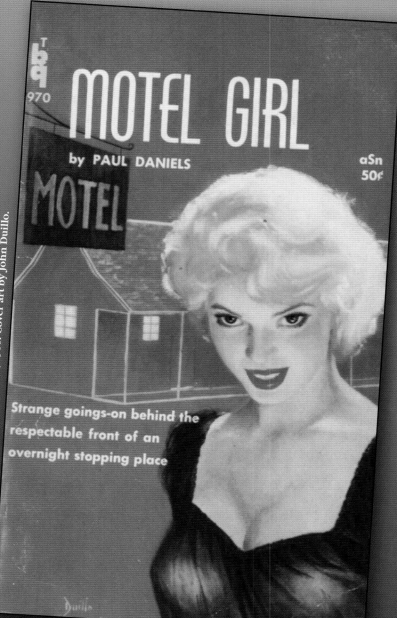

50¢ NOVEL BOOK 5068

FOR ADULTS

HUNGRY FOR MEN!

y were all between 18
25, beautifully built,
d hadn't had a man in
ee hundred days!

"publication preview
unforgettable
who have lived!"

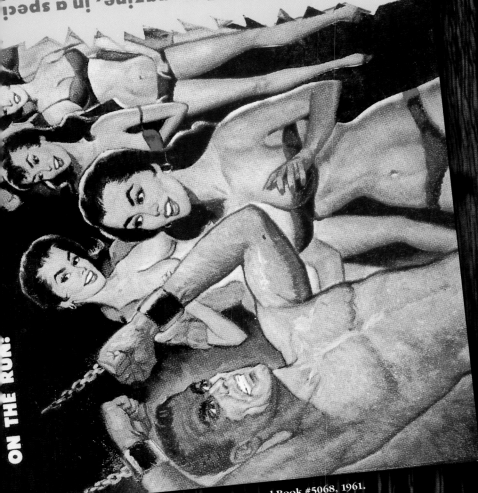

Hungry For Men! by Lou Fisher; Novel Book #5068, 1961.

BERKLEY BOOKS

G237

35¢

THEY POSED FOR THE BIG PAYOFF

SHOWROOM GIRLS

TOKEN WEST

Originally published as
CONQUERED

Young Kathy possessed a gorgeous figure whose lush charms she didn't mind displaying before the lustful eyes of lingerie buyers. Kathy soon discovered that with her exquisite face and body,

love was a highly marketable commodity...

Then she met the rich and sinister Vandine. In his arms, Kathy explored the bitter depths of unholy love...

Felice was hot, passionate, wild,
impossible, fantastic, incredible and
she loved men, real men—
but she also loved money…
Yes, she loved money. So it was up
to Jim, a man possessed by this half-
woman, half-animal to go out and get
it, even if it meant killing two men—
one her own husband…

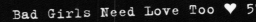

she was hot...
too hot for any one man

A TASTE FOR SIN

GIL BREWER

A BERKLEY ORIGINAL

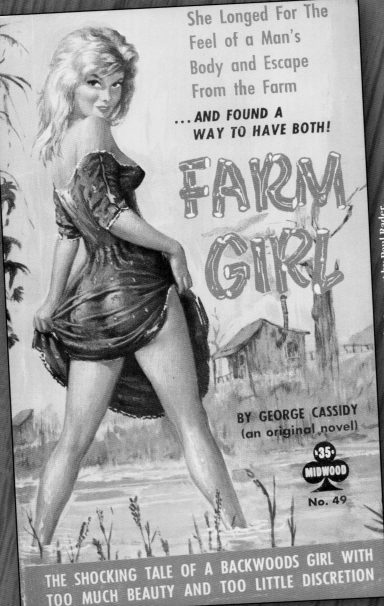

She Longed For The
Feel of a Man's
Body and Escape
From the Farm

...AND FOUND A
WAY TO HAVE BOTH!

FARM GIRL

BY GEORGE CASSIDY
(an original novel)

•35•
MIDWOOD

No. 49

THE SHOCKING TALE OF A BACKWOODS GIRL WITH
TOO MUCH BEAUTY AND TOO LITTLE DISCRETION

Farm Girl by George Cassidy; Midwood Book #49, 1960. Cover art by Paul Rader.

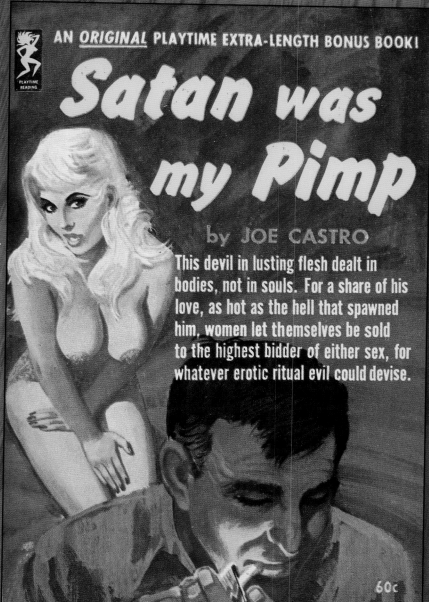

AN <u>ORIGINAL</u> PLAYTIME EXTRA-LENGTH BONUS BOOK!

Satan was my Pimp

by JOE CASTRO

This devil in lusting flesh dealt in bodies, not in souls. For a share of his love, as hot as the hell that spawned him, women let themselves be sold to the highest bidder of either sex, for whatever erotic ritual evil could devise.

60c

Satan Was My Pimp by Joe Castro; Playtime Book #660, 1964. Cover art by Robert Bonfils.

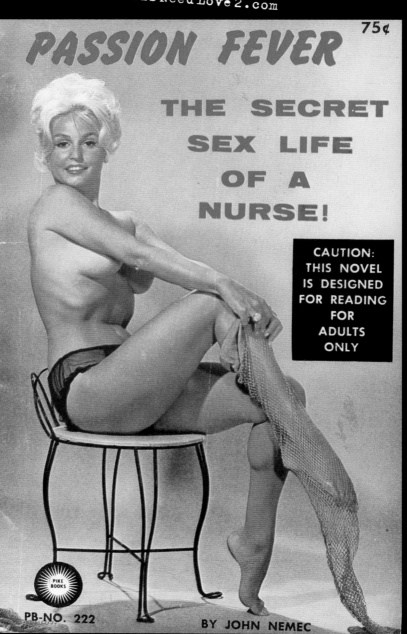

75¢

PASSION FEVER

THE SECRET SEX LIFE OF A NURSE!

CAUTION:
THIS NOVEL IS DESIGNED FOR READING FOR ADULTS ONLY

PIKE BOOKS

PB-NO. 222

BY JOHN NEMEC

Passion Fever by John Nemec; Pike Book #PB-222, 1963. Cover photo by Keith Bernard.

"Carol! Carol! You're so fantastic!"
He quickly reached for her. They
seized each other, hands seeking
and finding and caressing, as they
stumbled into the tile bathtub.
Carol battled him viciously and they
became two animals of lust.

When dames get tough anything can happen and usually does. I stretched out on the top of the bunk and began to think about this Julie dame. Was she curved, or was she curved? Her figure reminded me of a Coney Island roller coaster.

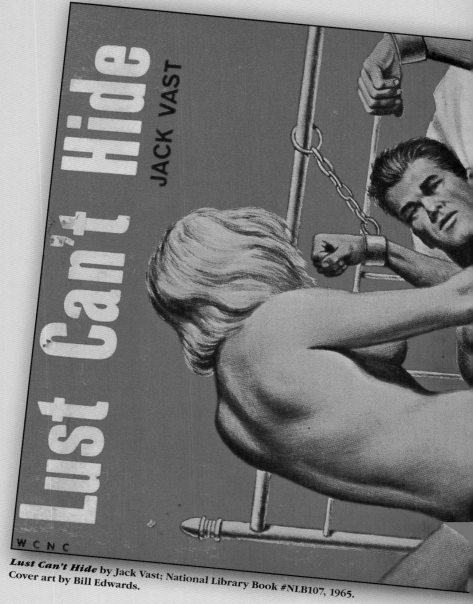

Lust Can't Hide by Jack Vast; National Library Book #NLB107, 1965.
Cover art by Bill Edwards.

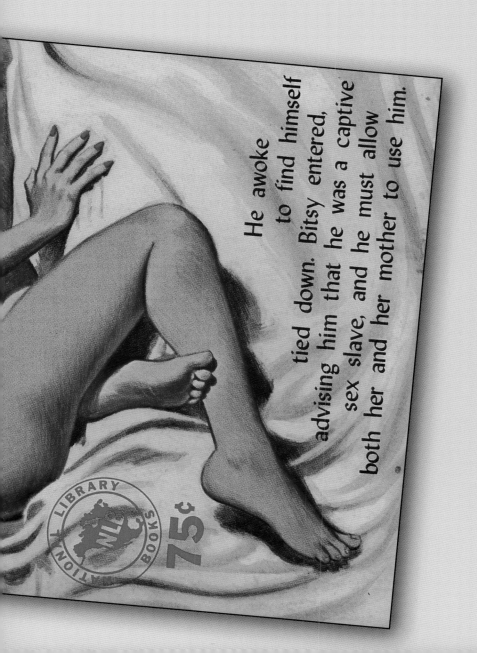

He awoke to find himself tied down. Bitsy entered, advising him that he was a captive sex slave, and he must allow both her and her mother to use him.

Kay was drinking a lot, more than she should, and she was frequently drunk. When she wasn't working or with Iris she would drink alone and it was then that a wave of disgust and self-pity assailed her. She was married to a man who didn't give a damn about her. She was a call girl. And, if that weren't enough, she was also a lesbian.

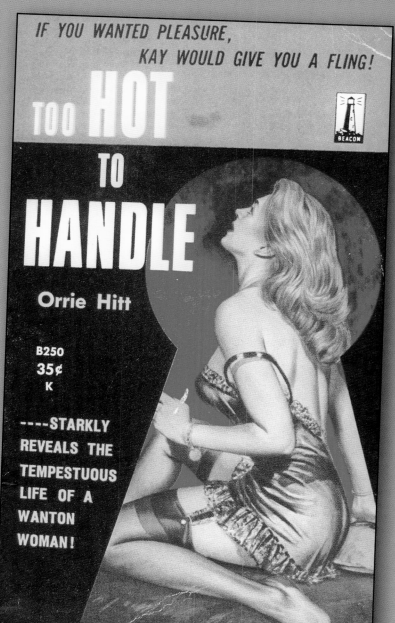

IF YOU WANTED PLEASURE,
KAY WOULD GIVE YOU A FLING!

TOO **HOT**
TO
HANDLE

Orrie Hitt

B250
35¢
K

----STARKLY
REVEALS THE
TEMPESTUOUS
LIFE OF A
WANTON
WOMAN!

BEACON

THEY WERE THE IN GROUP SWINGERS OF THE—

JET SET SWITCH

IH 502 ★ 75c

By JOHN DEXTER

AN IDLE HOUR BOOK

Jet Set Switch by John Dexter; Idle Hour Book #IH-502, 1966.

Susan lent a helping hand and began to play with Rocky's breasts, all the while flying higher on Bart's inspired flesh. Then everyone was very comfortable and very cozy at play, except that this was an adult game. A sensual game, a game of breasts and thighs and rubbing hands, a game of mouths and tongues, a game of vibrating flesh and palpitating bellies…

95c

any man's Playmate

by

RUBEL

the most delightfully shocking story you've ever read!

ADULT READING

TWO COMPLETE FULL LENGTH NOVELS!

Any Man's Playmate by James L. Rubel; Dollar Double Book #951, 1959. Cover art by Robert Bonfils.

ANY PORT IN A STORM — AND
ONE OF THE PORTS WAS LESBOS

the Drifter

K
50
MIDWOOD

NO. F163

By MARCH HASTINGS

She drifted from bed to bed,
from men to women, trying to
blot out pain with pleasure.

The Drifter by March Hastings; Midwood Book #F163, 1962. Cover art by Paul Rader.

DOMINO
BOOKS

72-728

LAS VEGAS MADAM

by MATT HARDING

**She ruled an empire of vice
—but her own twisted desires
made her a tortured slave**

Red light for lust!

And the hottest of them all was Linda, who ran a motel where the room service included all varieties of passion-for-pay…

It all made the job ten times tougher, but the fringe benefits were all female, all feverish, and all fabulous!

KOZY BOOK
K-172
50¢

BED
AND
BOARD

by Jonathon Ward

. . . the two girls
abandoned . . .
caressed . . . and
gestered . . . .

ADULT
READING

COZY UP WITH KOZY BOOKS

Bed and Board by Jonathon Ward; Kozy Book #K172, 1962.

Meet pretty Deedy Harmon, a delight to party with—and dynamite to love.

THIRD BIG PRINTING!

BLONDE TRAP

by Ernie Weatherall

SOFT COVER LIBRARY

B851X
60¢
K

THE STORY OF A SULTRY OFFICE GIRL
WHO BELIEVED IN **PLEASURE BEFORE BUSINESS!**

Blonde Trap by Ernie Weatherall; Softcover Library #B851X, 1965.

Still laughing, she let her fingers go to work. They tweaked and titillated as if the red nails dripped sweet acid. Then her lips, red and luscious and perfumed as a flower, got busy. It was like fire trickling over my skin. I groaned. The pleasure was so acute it was almost unbearable. "I'm going to give you an extra-special treat," murmured Deedy. "Then later you can do the same for me…"

The Invaders by Anthony Dean; After Hours Book #AH138, 1966. Cover art by Gene Bilbrew.

As Lon moved forward, feeling the shag rug on his bare feet, he was aware of the pounding in his veins, his rock hard powers in pointed urgency. He felt his face burn. Hell, he really did feel as if he were in another century, being led around in his Nature suit, while every girl in the area could do what she wanted with him. When was this going to end!

Gloria lay down on the bed. Dan started to take off her dress, kissing her. She needed him, had to have him. She pulled his lips down to cover hers, and shivered with delight…
It was then that Gloria became aware of Helen's hands on her, too! There were four hands coming at her from all sides, all over her. She let passion ride, soar…for a moment aware of sensation, of flesh against flesh.

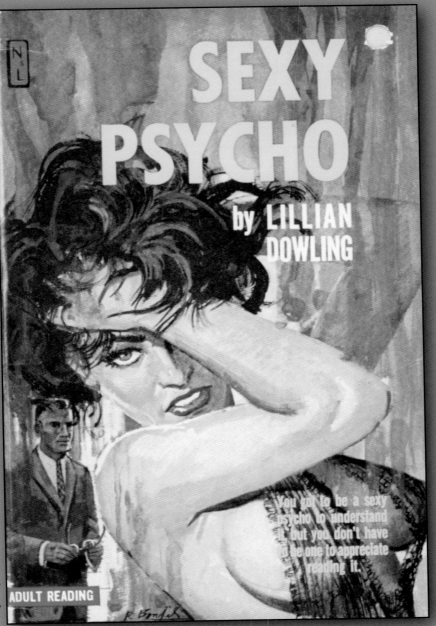

SEXY PSYCHO

by LILLIAN DOWLING

ADULT READING

You got to be a sexy psycho to understand it, but you don't have to be one to appreciate reading it.

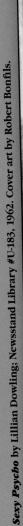

Sexy Psycho by Lillian Dowling; Newsstand Library #U-183, 1962. Cover art by Robert Bonfils.

A SEETHING TURMOIL OF PASSION, VIOLENCE AND HATRED

FALCON No. 40 PDC

WHIP-HAND!

ANOTHER
BRAND NEW NOVEL
BY **HODGE EVENS**

Author of "YELLOWHEAD"

and "THREE FOR PASSION"

35c

A FALCON BOOK

Whip-Hand! by Hodge Evens; Falcon Book #40, 1952, digest-sized paperback.

Margo flicked the quirt against her leg and said, "I'm going to whip off your dress. Then I'm going to cut your under things. I'm going to make you come crawling to me on your hands and knees. A whipping hurts." She smiled. "I've kept this whip on purpose."

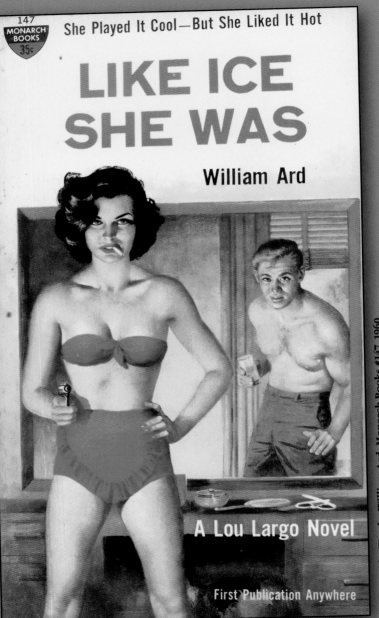

She Played It Cool—But She Liked It Hot

LIKE ICE SHE WAS

William Ard

A Lou Largo Novel

First Publication Anywhere

Like Ice She Was by William Ard; Monarch Books #147, 1960.

BAD GIRL
abroad

50¢

Madelaine wanted love,
the American way, with
a marriage band—but the
men she met in Europe
just wanted MADELAINE . . .

ARTHUR ADLON

Woman in the Window by Jack Moore; Saber Book #SA-89, 1965. Cover art by Bill Edwards.

Jerry had watched her from the time she was fully dressed, till she stood majestically nude before his hungry eyes. Could he get at her? He found a way!

SABER BOOK 75¢

Blanche got me started. Blanche with her stunning clothes and silver foxes that cost more than I could earn in a year waiting tables.

"A girl as young and good looking as you, Dorine, is a fool to waste her time like this. Let me teach you the ropes. I'll see you started right."

That night I made thirty five dollars.

21
PB
PYRAMID BOOKS

(Scarlet Patrol)

SIN STREET

The inside story of the vice racket as told by a Call Girl!

JOE'S

"The most fascinating book I have read and, perhaps, as a portrait of today's unknown life, the truest"
— G. S. FIORDALISI, Observer to United Nations White Slavery Committee.

DORINE MANNERS

COMPLETE AND UNABRIDGED

25¢

Sin Street by Dorine Manners; Pyramid Book #21, 1950.

Kitty made time with the boss behind his wife's back — and with everybody else behind the boss's back!

POUND OF FLESH

Simms Albert

BEACON

B 287

35¢

K

A NOVEL WHICH AT LAST TELLS THE TRUTH ABOUT THOSE OFFICE GIRLS WHOSE CHIEF BUSINESS ASSETS ARE THEIR BODIES...

Pound of Flesh by Simms Albert; Beacon Book #B287, 1960.

She didn't consider herself a prostitute...!

A croaking laugh of derision escaped his lips. "You're cheap, Kitty," he growled. There was lashing contempt in his voice. "You're cheap as dirt."

PDC

EXOTIC NOVEL

PROFUSELY ILLUSTRATED

OCT.

35c

THRILL GIRL!

AN ORIGINAL UNCENSORED NOVEL BY

Gene Harvey

Author of the sensational best seller, "PASSION'S SLAVE!"

ONE MAN WASN'T ENOUGH

Exotic Novel, 1950, digest-size paperback.

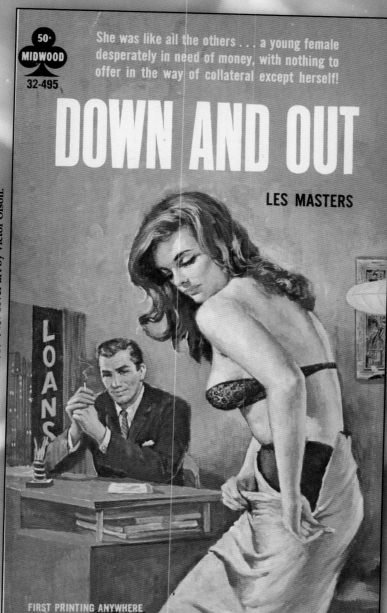

She was like all the others . . . a young female desperately in need of money, with nothing to offer in the way of collateral except herself!

50¢

MIDWOOD ♣

32-495

DOWN AND OUT

LES MASTERS

LOANS

FIRST PRINTING ANYWHERE

Down and Out by Les Masters; Midwood Book #32-495, 1965. Cover art by Victor Olson.

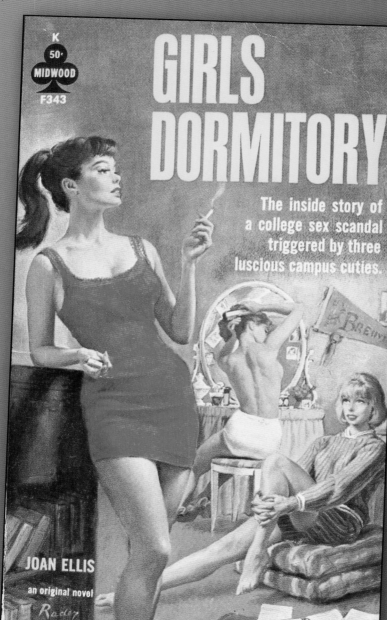

Elaine, cute and cuddly, she learned the easiest and fastest way to earn passing grades from her male professors.

Adele, older and wiser, she paid her way through school with the money she'd earned as a very special kind of party girl.

Mona, sleek and sensuous, she was as popular with her sorority sisters as she was with the campus wolves…and for the same reason.

Joyce liked working for Lingerie
Ltd. But it seemed that in return for
advancement she was expected
to confer her favors upon the men
around the place. They could
not know that Joyce had an
unwholesome aversion to members
of the male species. She reserved
her affections for one of the young
secretaries, pert and adorable Doris.

Can a girl in the lingerie racket keep
her decency even while she
sheds her clothes?

BEACON

B300

LINGERIE LTD.

RALPH DEAN

35¢

K

A bold, brilliant book — pitilessly revealing the
strange temptations besetting two attractive career
girls in a business without scruples!

LUSH DONNIE LEE DID NOT INTEND TO BE A DECEIVING WIFE ...SHE ONLY WANTED TO OCCUPY ...

the bed

BEACON
B477F
50¢
K

The Bed at the Top by Charles Beck; Beacon Book #B477F, 1962.

at the top

CHARLES BECK

YELLOW-HAIR HAD AN IN-
SATIABLE APPETITE FOR
MEN—FOR MONEY! SHE
MEANT TO HAVE HER FILL
OF BOTH, AND WAS PRE-
PARED TO PAY ANY PRICE
—WITH HER BODY!

NEVER BEFORE PUBLISHED

75

 PLAYTIME READING

Dance-Hall
DYKE

by
Toni
Adler

The vicious jungle
of lesbian lures
...the fickle and
the fake screaming
the obscenity of
their passions,
while tender lovers
cry for understanding

As Alicia bent to take a glass
from the cabinet, Kim grasped her
shoulders and jerked her up, abruptly.
Then Kim's mouth was on her lips.
Alicia's mind exploded in shock and
bewilderment.
"You're a lesbian!" Anger flushed her
face. "How dare you even think of me
this way?"
Kim's hands darted out and swiftly
pinned Alicia's arms to her sides.
"You're going to love me," Kim
whispered.

STAR
NOVELS

Hollywood
Hellcat

(Bedtime Blonde)

by John Underwood

No. 764
35¢

THE SHOCKING STORY OF WHAT A WOMAN MUST DO TO BECOME A STAR

She had everything all figured out:
A woman must use every weapon
she has at her disposal,
and sex is the strongest…
Make a sucker out of every man you can
because if you don't, he'll make a
sucker out of you.

She lay back, breasts floating, hair swirling in soft eddies around her beautiful face.

"Be big," she pleaded.

"Be—be a seahorse with a beard of Neptune and the strength of a shark! Hurt me, Brent! Oh, make me scream with hurt and want and hurt again!"

Satana by Helene Morgan; Rapture Book #RB303, 1964.

SATAN'S HARVEST

SANFORD ADAY

When Lupe saw Ramon
she knew she'd been
sold into sin

A FABIAN
ORIGINAL
NOVEL

35¢

He watched her flesh quiver,

while her stomach rose and fell with her breathing. He kissed it and then started to turn away. She put her hands gently on his head, trying to keep his lips against her flesh. He jerked his head up angrily and looked at her.

"Are you one of those freaks, Lupe?" His eyes were bulging with amazement and dismay.

"All men kiss women's stomachs," she said. 'That's the way people make love."

SHE LEARNED HER TRICKS AT THE BOTTOM OF
THE HEAP — AND HE WAS HER TICKET TO THE TOP!

OFFICE AFFAIR

MARK WEST

B421Y
40¢
K

When a Girl Friday makes
the grade in business, she
usually does her best work
after office hours . . . !

Office Affair by Mark West; Beacon Book #B421Y, 1961.

Janice put her body on the block as —
The PAYOFF
She made the first payment in his office

MIDWOOD
F232

By MAX COLLIER
author of "THORN OF EVIL"

FIRST PRINTING ANYWHERE

BITCH on WHEELS

by Robert Devlin

50¢

I've got the 'equipment' and I've got the plan . . . Now for the man . . .

DARLENE USED HER WILD, UNCONTROLLABLE PASSIONS TO JUMP FROM A TEXAS SHACK TO THE PLUSH LINED BEDS OF BIG CITY VICE . . .

Bitch on Wheels by Robert Devlin; Chariot Books #CB156, 1960.

Cynthia, too, was a winner, and liked to be associated with winners. Also she was vengeful. She would get even with Ross Baxter for having stood her up today if it was the last act of her life. She would ask him over here and she would wear her new white negligee with practically nothing at all under it. When her father came in and found her, quite probably, adorning Ross Baxter's lap, Baxter would suddenly find himself chucked bodily out of the house. Then that dime-a-dozen Casanova would learn who he could stand up and who he could not.

B449 F
50¢
K

He had Blanche at home and Kay in town —
the perfect arrangement until Cynthia came along.
She was bewitchingly beautiful, young
enough to be his daughter and hungry for the
thrills an older man could give her...

LOVE NOW
PAY LATER

BY ELAINE DORIAN

487
MONARCH BOOKS 50¢

A High Voltage Story Of Violence And Vice
Among Over-Privileged Teen-Agers

RUN TOUGH, RUN HARD

Carson Bingham

First Publication Anywhere

Run Tough, Run Hard by Carson Bingham; Monarch Book #487, 1964. Cover at by Ray Johnson.

Brad felt the warmth of Deedee's
body, the silkiness of her flesh and
the touch of her searching lips.
"I hate my mother," she sighed, "for
trying to steal you from me."
That was when the spotlight caught
them, stabbing through the darkness
at their near-nakedness. And behind
the spotlight was Lieutenant Pierce
of the Juvenile Bureau.

Gwen combined lush allure with a realistic capacity for getting what she wanted. By artful distribution of her kisses and other favors, she bound numerous men to her. But despite her many lovers she never lost sight of the great love of her life—herself!

THE MURDER OF A HUSSY

DEATH *is a* LOVELY LADY

RUTH FENISONG

Free and Easy by Luther Gordon; Ecstasy Novel #1, 1951, digest-size paperback.

PDC

NEVER Say "NO!"

(SATAN RULES THE NIGHT)

35c

No. 10

By *Luther Gordon*

Author of ILLICIT WIFE

ECSTASY
NOVEL

SHE WAS BEAUTIFUL

HELL'S HARLOT

She was all woman—all tramp!

By DON HOLLIDAY

Her body was a flame
that fed on men . . .

MAN
TRAP

Lora was eighteen —
and too hot to be handled:
—by the stepfather
who wanted to ruin her
—by the lover
who wanted to maul her
—by the man
who wanted to love her

BEACON

B360
35¢
K

MATT
HARDING

60c

PLAYTIME
READING

ATOMIC BLONDE

by MONTE STEELE

She dealt in hot cars
her own hot flesh –
and would throw in a
taste of disaster
for good measure

Atomic Blonde by Monte Steele; Playtime Books #639, 1963. Cover art by Robert Bonfils.

We grew more frenzied.

She shuddered as waves of ecstasy raced through her body, exciting me in return. Her heels dug into my rump as she wiggled and pivoted violently upon the bed.

And then it was too much for both of us and we exploded together. I bit her shoulder in the final shattering spasm and fell to the side, still holding her in my arms. We lay for a long time together, limp and gasping for breath.

She Couldn't Love Men
—So She Turned To Women

MIDWOOD

k 50¢
No. 63

The Unfortunate Flesh

By RANDY SALEM
(an original novel)

A TOUCHING STORY OF THE THIRD SEX AND FORBIDDEN LOVE

The Unfortunate Flesh by Randy Salem; Midwood Books #63, 1960. Cover art by Paul Rader.

BY GEORGE H. SMITH

THIRST FOR LOVE

FOR ADULTS

She was built—but she was proud—until her perverted husband and the cancer of socialism drove her to the heights of a shameless nymphomania

Thirst For Love by George H. Smith; Novel Book #6013, 1962.

She came to him with a rutting-bitch-dog abandon!

With the terrible power of a naked-bladed bulldozer. She laid warm hands on her own pendulous breasts, rubbed them to an almost unbearable demanding, then she closed her eyes…sooty lashes batting, batting… mocking him!…tempting him!… trapping him!

Imprisoned desires and frustrated love behind the walls of a woman's reformatory-school fester into a seething hot-bed of unleashed passions and vice. None of the unfortunate women are able to escape this web of lustful sins that are forced upon them by their fellow prisoners because they are inmates in a...sin-infested, hell hole!

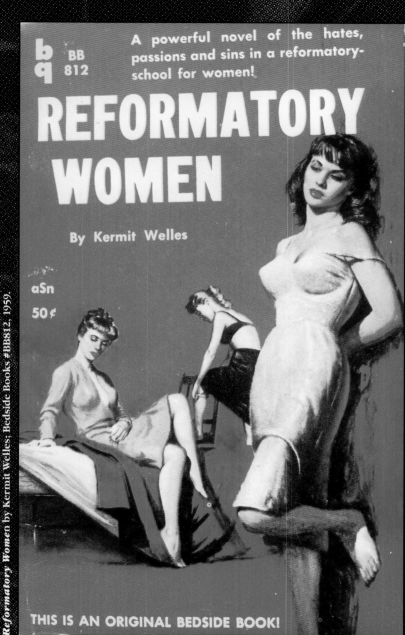

BB
812

bq

A powerful novel of the hates, passions and sins in a reformatory-school for women!

REFORMATORY WOMEN

By Kermit Welles

aSn

50¢

THIS IS AN ORIGINAL BEDSIDE BOOK!

VERY PRIVATE SECRETARY

HIS WIFE WAS CHEATING...

HIS SECRETARY

WAS BEWITCHING...

AVAILABLE...

WILLING!

A NOVEL
WHICH BOLDLY,
CANDIDLY PORTRAYS
THE ROLE OF
THE OFFICE WIFE
IN BIG BUSINESS
TODAY.

by Jack Hanley

BEACON

B296
35¢
K

Very Private Secretary by Jack Hanley; Beacon Books #B296, 1960.

She sighed, stretching her provocative body sinuously, aware of David's eyes on her. And then his hands were slipping over the polished shoulders, drawing her closer to him. She held still, suffering his hands on her body and his kiss on her closed lips, then a low laugh sounded deep in her throat. "You were a good boy to do as I asked you. Now the good boy wants his reward, doesn't he?" she cooed.

STRANGERS IN EVERY WAY — BUT ONE!

NIGHT
OF
SHAME

Lewis Lester

BEACON

B 234

35¢ K

A NOVEL OF LOVE BECOME CORRUPTION —
OF TWO WHO KNEW EACH OTHER'S BODIES,
BUT NOT EACH OTHER'S NAMES...

Night of Shame by Lewis Lester; Beacon Books #B234, 1959.

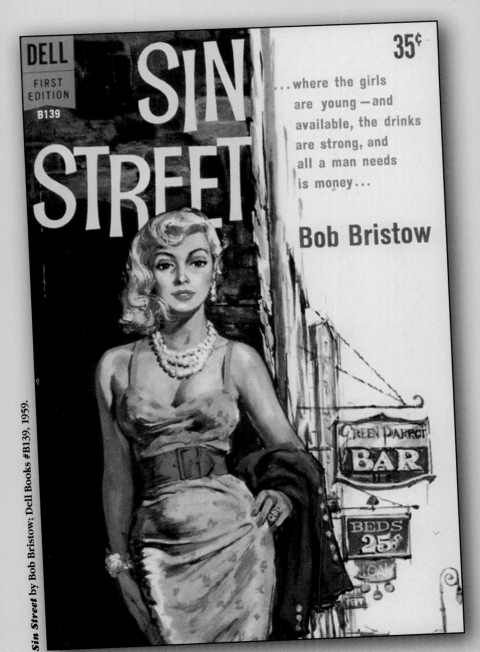

She moved her body against his,
pressing herself close.
He wanted to grab her in his arms.
More than anything else he wanted
his arms crushing her as tightly as he
could. In that flash of time he knew
what would happen…

It would be heaven and hell and thunder and lightning and hurricane.

He could smell the good warm odor
of her. It blotted out everything else.

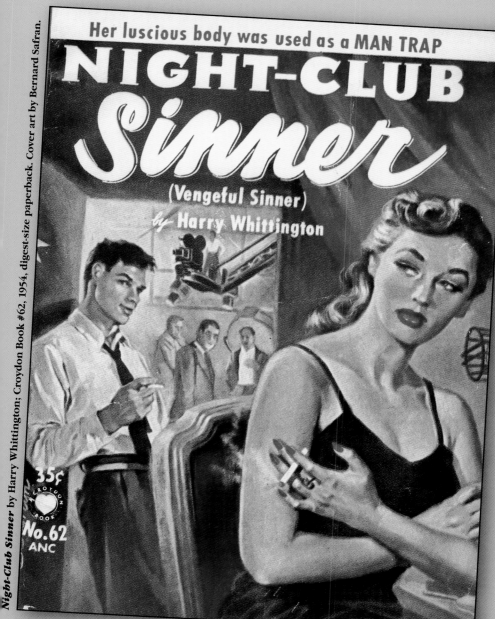

Her luscious body was used as a MAN TRAP

NIGHT-CLUB

Sinner

(Vengeful Sinner)

by Harry Whittington

35¢

CROYDON BOOK

No. 62
ANC

THIS IS A BITING BOOK. IN ITS SIZZLING PAGES, EVERY CAREER GIRL WILL RECOGNIZE HERSELF—OR SOMEONE SHE KNOWS!

BACHELOR GIRL

"Without clothes you don't look like a secretary," he whispered.

But he was wrong.

In her circle, it was the proper "uniform" for an ambitious career girl....

FRANCIS LOREN

Bachelor Girl by Frances Loren; Beacon Signal Book #B583F, 1963.
Cover art by Robert Maguire.

SHE COULDN'T CONTROL HER STRANGE EMOTIONS!

WILD HUNGER

by Fred Malloy

BEACON

B171
35¢
K

THE STORY OF SUSAN
—WHO WANTED MORE,
AND WOULD DO ANYTHING TO GET IT . . . .

Wild Hunger by Fred Malloy; Beacon Books #B171, 1958.

His knee pressed harder into her back, as he leaned to grasp a handful of her flimsy blouse. He tore the entire back out of it in a single sweeping motion.

"There, you hussy, how do you like that?"

Diane had an unlimited appetite for
sex, in all of its many forms—
and enough money to maintain a
captive harem of males to satisfy
her every twisted desire!
Robert was willing to try anything
once, but being the love-slave of a
beautiful woman wasn't quite his
idea of the right way to go wrong!

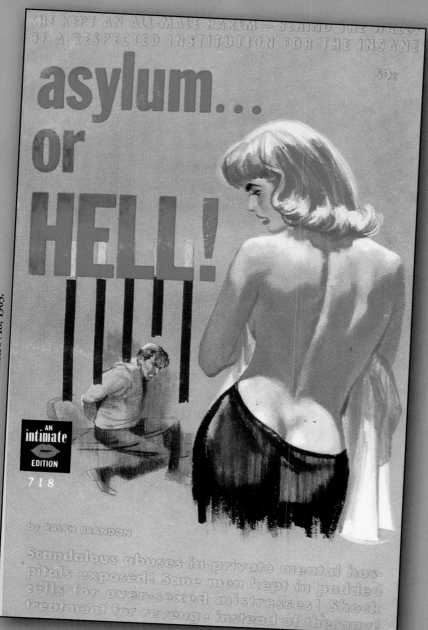

SHE KEPT AN ALL-MALE HAREM — BEHIND THE WALLS
OF A RESPECTED INSTITUTION FOR THE INSANE

asylum...
or
HELL!

50¢

AN
intimate
EDITION

7 1 8

by RALPH BRANDON

Scandalous abuses in private mental hospitals exposed! Sane men kept in padded cells for over-sexed mistresses! Shock treatment for revenge instead of therapy!

THREE LOVERS WERE NOT ENOUGH FOR THESE GIRLS!

KEPT SISTERS

Florence Stonebraker

The story of sisters
so love-hungry
they shared
the same sins—
the same delights—
THE SAME MEN!

B388
35¢
K

BEACON

Kept Sisters by Florence Stonebraker; Beacon Book #B388, 1961.

NO RECENT NOVEL HAS DARED TO GO SO FAR
IN EXPOSING IMMORALITY AMONG "NICE" PEOPLE

SHE COULD TANTALIZE AND TEASE—
BUT SHE KNEW HOW TO PLEASE...

HELL BENT

by H. B. Ames

B 163
35¢
K

Hell Bent by H. B. Ames; Beacon Book #B163, 1958.

THE STORY OF JOAN, WHO
LOVED HER WAY OUT OF
THE GUTTER—AND BACK!

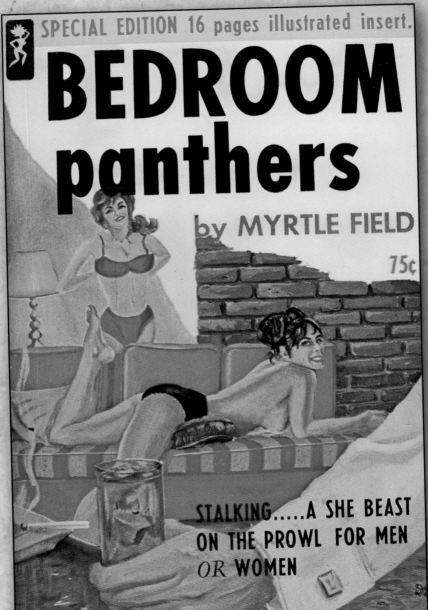

SPECIAL EDITION 16 pages illustrated insert.

BEDROOM
panthers

by MYRTLE FIELD

75¢

STALKING.....A SHE BEAST
ON THE PROWL FOR MEN
OR WOMEN

Bedroom Panthers by Myrtle Field; Playtime Book #716-S, 1965.

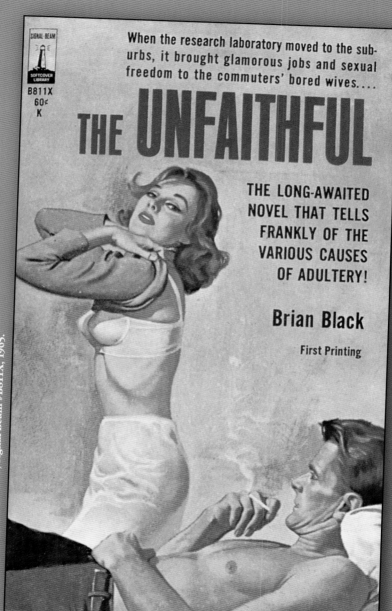

When the research laboratory moved to the sub-
urbs, it brought glamorous jobs and sexual
freedom to the commuters' bored wives....

THE UNFAITHFUL

THE LONG-AWAITED
NOVEL THAT TELLS
FRANKLY OF THE
VARIOUS CAUSES
OF ADULTERY!

Brian Black

First Printing

SIGNAL BEAM

SOFTCOVER
LIBRARY

B811X
60¢
K

The Unfaithful by Brian Black; Signal Beam #B811X, 1965.

A queer little thrill shot through me, a strange delicious warmth that tickled delightfully and made my breath catch in my throat. I waited a few moments; then, in a mousy, apologetic voice, I said, "Would you... slap me like that again, Patricia? That felt kind of... well... kind of nice."

She didn't answer. But she did as I'd asked. A little harder this time. But still playfully. And instantly a "playful" thrill trickled through me and made me catch my breath again.

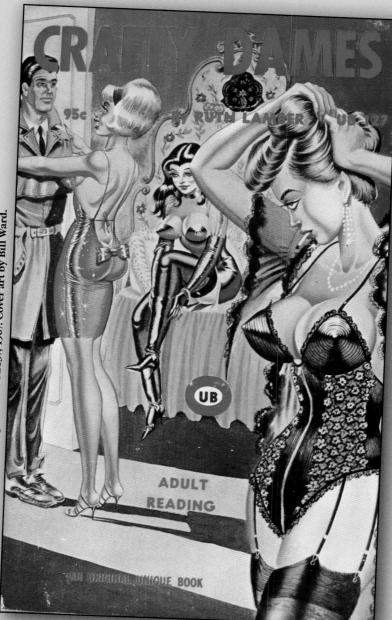

Crafty Dames by Ruth Lamber; Unique Book #UB137, 1967. Cover art by Bill Ward.

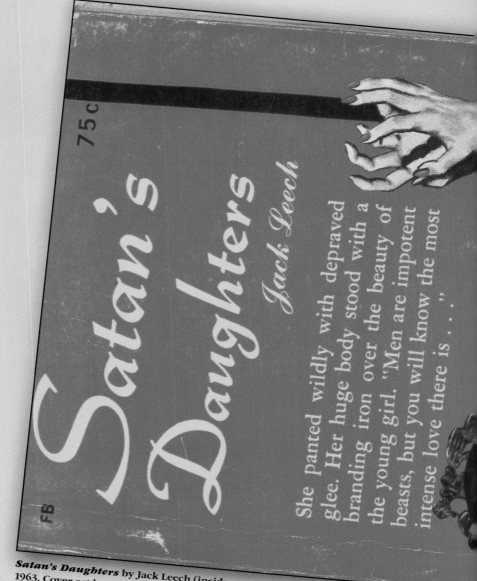

75c

FB

Satan's Daughters

Jack Leech

She panted wildly with depraved glee. Her huge body stood with a branding iron over the beauty of the young girl. "Men are impotent beasts, but you will know the most intense love there is . . . ."

Satan's Daughters by Jack Leech (inside says by Jack Trimble); Europa Book #1104, 1963. Cover art by Bill Edwards.

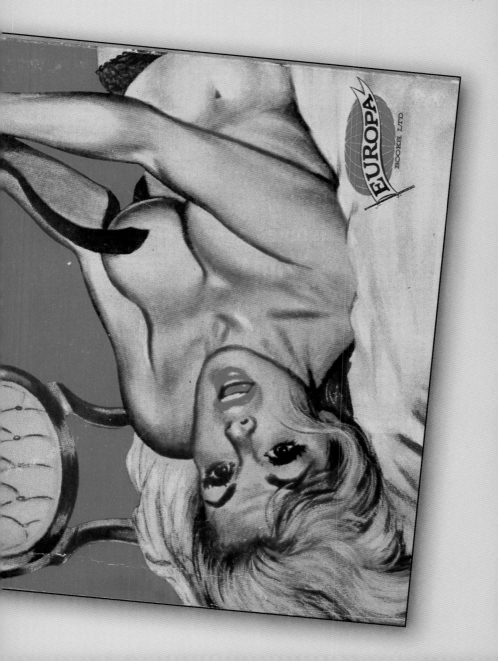

Martha's legs were strong, her sinuous hips tick-tocking in growing rhythm with the silken insistence of her thighs.

"Hurt me,"

she hissed, "hurt me," and he had tried to ignore the ragged urgency of her voice. Until she forced him to listen. With slashing fingernails across his back; with animal teeth that tore at his mouth.

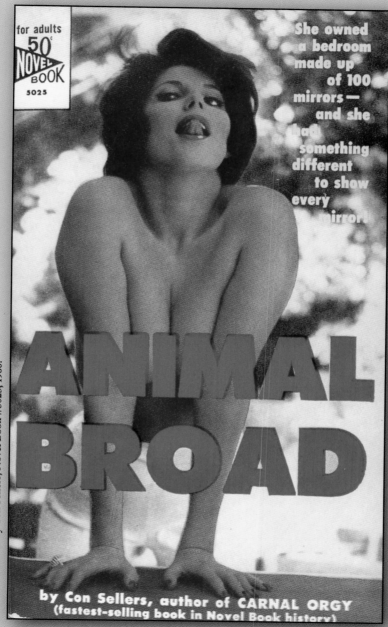

for adults
50¢
NOVEL BOOK
5025

She owned
a bedroom
made up
of 100
mirrors—
and she
had
something
different
to show
every
mirror

ANIMAL
BROAD

by Con Sellers, author of CARNAL ORGY
(fastest-selling book in Novel Book history)

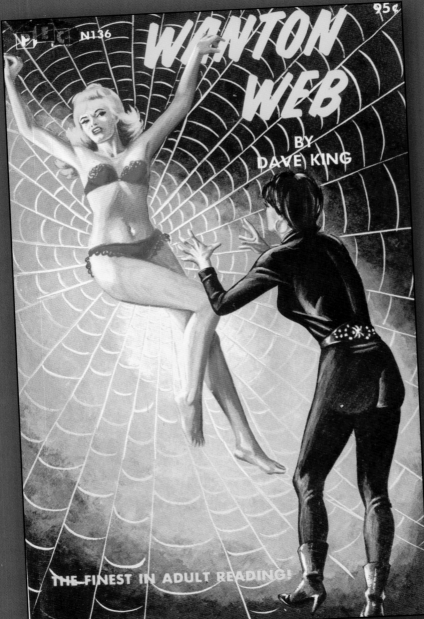

Paul, Hollywood publicity man, went
to a party…and was shocked to find
he was the only guest with clothes on!
Paul resolved to cut out and stay
out. It wasn't his type bash. Then,
somebody burgled his apartment…
beautiful girls, who'd been at the
undressed party, dropped in to
inflame him with tastes of love.

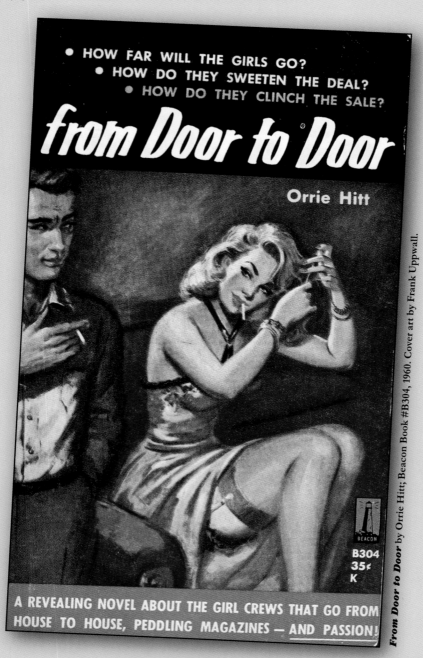

- HOW FAR WILL THE GIRLS GO?
- HOW DO THEY SWEETEN THE DEAL?
- HOW DO THEY CLINCH THE SALE?

from Door to Door

Orrie Hitt

B304
35¢
K

A REVEALING NOVEL ABOUT THE GIRL CREWS THAT GO FROM HOUSE TO HOUSE, PEDDLING MAGAZINES — AND PASSION!

From Door to Door by Orrie Hitt; Beacon Book #B304, 1960. Cover art by Frank Uppwall.

STREET of DARK DESIRES

A BRAND-NEW, UNCENSORED NOVEL
By MARK REED

Author of
FOUR DAMES
NAMED "SIN"

A NOVEL OF
WOMEN WHO KISS . . . BUT
NEVER FOR LOVE!

PDC

35¢

NO. 107

Part woman, part lusting animal,

Hazel could take the abuse men dished out, as long as it brought her more excitement, added success, increased riches. And by the time the seductive beauty had finished with the men at her command, she had what she always wanted—plus some things she could do without!

Harlot in Her Heart by Norman Bligh; Ecstasy Novel, 1950. Cover art by Jean Claude Rodewald.

THE LADY IS A LUSH

Where does the cocktail hour lead wives like Amy—who can't stop with one drink?

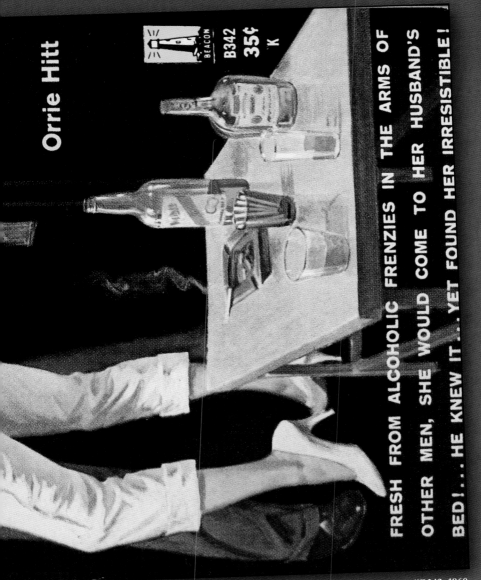

Orrie Hitt

BEACON
B342
35¢
K

FRESH FROM ALCOHOLIC FRENZIES IN THE ARMS OF OTHER MEN, SHE WOULD COME TO HER HUSBAND'S BED!...HE KNEW IT...YET FOUND HER IRRESISTIBLE!

The Lady is a Lush by Orrie Hitt; Beacon Book #B342; 1960.

G30

Half-wanton, half witch,
she ruled a French prison!

SHE-
DEVIL

"Strong meat . . . bawdy . . .
eminently readable!"
—*New York Herald Tribune*

Harry Hervey

(Original Title: The Iron Widow)

35c

"Break him!" she screamed.
Two burly guards pushed him against
the wall, pinning him there. Each time
she gave the order, they struck him.
He wanted to cry out. He prayed that
he might faint. But beyond them he
could see her—the woman who had
shared his bed only nights before, her
eyes gleaming now with pleasure at
his torment.

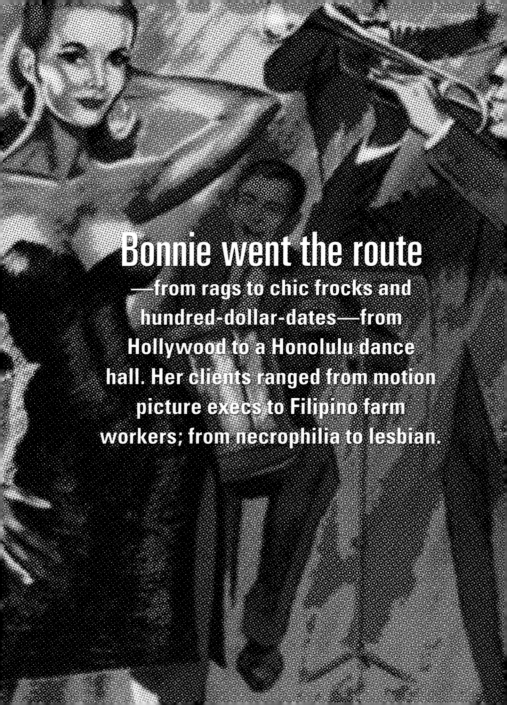

Bonnie went the route

—from rags to chic frocks and hundred-dollar-dates—from Hollywood to a Honolulu dance hall. Her clients ranged from motion picture execs to Filipino farm workers; from necrophilia to lesbian.

Dime-A-Dance Hustler by Eve Linkletter; PEC #N-141, 1966.

OUT OF DARKNESS

by LONNY BASS

It took longer than six years, and a good woman, to dissuade Carl from his contention that Sex was abnormal and indecent.

SABER BOOK 35¢

SHE WAS FAIR...SHE WAS FRISKY...
SHE WAS OH, SUCH FUN...

CALL HER WANTON

by Lon Williams

35¢

A LUSTY NOVEL OF WILDERNESS PASSION AND A WIFE TOO NAUGHTY TO BE TRUE!

A BEACON FIRST AWARD ORIGINAL

Call Her Wanton by Lon Williams; Beacon Book #BB149, 1957. Cover art by Saul Levine.

FALCON NO. 44
PDC

Honky Tonk Girl

A BRAND NEW,
UNCENSORED
UNEXPURGATED
NOVEL BY
CHARLES BECKMAN, JR

IT WAS THE LAST STOP FOR THE SCUM OF HUMANITY ON THE ROAD TO HELL!

35c

Honky Tonk Girl by Charles Beckman, Jr. Falcon Book #44, 1953, digest-size paperback.

Somewhere along Honky Tonk Street, hidden beneath the slime and filth and misery, there are three beautiful women — and Johnny knows that one of them holds the key to Miff's death.

Is it Ruth, so innocent and loving, Ruth — whose body remembers more than her mind cares to admit?

Or is it Jean, the ravishing — and too often ravished — beauty?

Or can it be Raye, the nymphomaniac and part-time handmaiden of violence?

A SHOCKING STORY OF LIVES AND FEMALE
DESIRES WARPED BEYOND REASON BY A
CRUEL AND SADISTIC IDEA OF JUSTICE

WOMEN IN PRISON

35¢
MIDWOOD
NO. 120

Women in Prison by Mike Avallone; Midwood Book #120, 1961. Cover art by Paul Rader.

"You're a stranger and I'm not only letting you kiss me but I'm kissing you, too."
"Is that so bad?"
"Not the kissing, but where it leads."
"And where does it lead?"
"Do I have to put it into words?"
"Yeah."
She did and the next time she moaned and twisted in my arms. She pressed closer and her teeth cut into my lower lip. I tasted blood and I heard the dress rip.
"The bedroom," she whispered.

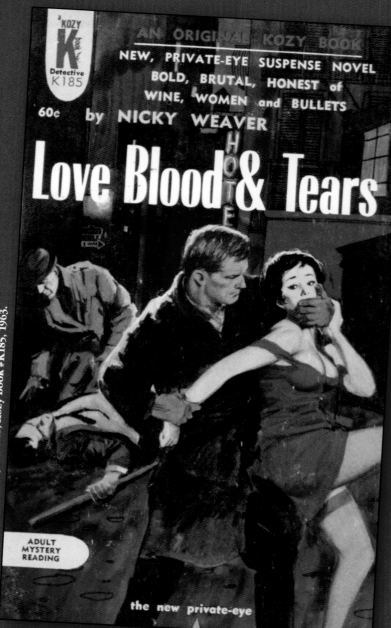

WCNC

First Edition

SWINGERS IN DANGER

DREW
PALMER

SABER

BOOK
$1.25

She was a beautiful Negress.
He was white. She wanted the
apartment. He wanted her.
Time for integration. . .

Swingers in Danger by Drew Palmer; Saber Book #SA-135, 1968. Cover art probably by Bill Edwards.

Every student majored in Sex and Vice at

SIN SCHOOL

By DON
HOLLIDAY

K 35¢

AN ORIGINAL
NOVEL

MIDWOOD

What The Students
Learned In This
School Of Hell
NO BOOK EVER TAUGHT!

Sin School by Don Holliday; Midwood Book #25, 1959.

Blonde, voluptuous Betsy was a singer with a big-name band

— she didn't mean to be bad, she just couldn't help it...

Neglected by her handsome husband Don and surrounded by admiring males, she found the days and nights on the road a living hell of thwarted desires...

Betsy tried desperately to control her yearning, but one night in the arms of Don's best friend she learned that sin can be satisfying.

He was out for the big deals, and she was his...

Bait

GEORGE CASSIDY

Melody covered the convention front — as a "special assistant" — and swung those big deals in her own way!

BEACON
SIGNAL

B525F

50¢

K

A NOVEL THAT DARES TO REVEAL HOW WOMEN ARE USED AS PAWNS IN TODAY'S WORLD OF HIGH FINANCE!

Bait by George Cassidy; Beacon Book #B525F, 1962. Cover art by "Gida."

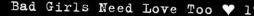

60c

FEMALE PEEPING TOM

by BILL ADAMS

She was an expose
reporter who would
do anything for a
story...it helped
to be sexy looking

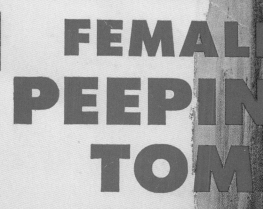

The PLATINUM TRAP

K
50¢
MIDWOOD
F202

From the tip of her toes
to her platinum top
Joan Browne's body was
a devouring trap
that fed her greed
for fame and pleasure.

By MIKE AVALLONE

FIRST PRINTING ANYWHERE

MAN OR WOMAN, SISTER OR BROTHER: HER LUST KNEW NO BOUNDS!

THE NEEDLE

SLOANE M. BRITAIN

B 237
35¢
K

BEACON

PITILESSLY EXPOSES THE DEPRAVITY
OF THE TRUE ADDICT, WHO TAKES LOVERS
WITHOUT NUMBER, PERFORMS EVERY
HEINOUS VICE, IN ORDER TO EMBRACE HER
ONE TRUE LOVE....THE NEEDLE!

The Needle by Sloane M. Britain, Beacon Books #B237, 1959.

A scorching story of a beautiful teen-age girl who tried to escape the sweat and lust of the teeming tenements—and raised herself from the gutter to a better life. She used her lovely body as bait and landed some of the "big fish" from the muddy waters of big business lust!

CB-217

50¢

HUNGRY LIPS — SUBMISSIVE FLESH.
WAS SHE A YOUNG TRAMP? WAS SHE
THRILL HUNGRY?
OR WAS SHE
JUST—

MAN BAIT

by
**ALEXIS
ROGET**

Man Bait by Alexis Roget; Chariot Book #CB217, 1962.

WB 104
75c
ONE NIGHT A
TEEN AGED
VIRGIN . . .
THE NEXT
NIGHT . . .
THE
QUEEN
OF THE

KOOCH
DANCERS

BY
HERN FELD

ADULTS
ONLY

THIS IS AN ORIGINAL WING BOOK

The Queen of the Kooch Dancers by Hern Feld; Wing Book #WB-104, 1965.

FOR THE PRICE OF A TICKET, YOU COULD
ENJOY RHONDA'S CHARMS...

CARNIVAL GIRL

Orrie Hitt

B238
35¢ K

A BEHIND-THE-SCENES GLIMPSE OF
TENT-SHOW LIFE — OF THE TAWDRY GLAMOR,
THE SORDID LUST, THE SINS AND THE SCANDALS
OF GIRLS TRAINED TO PLEASE!

Carnival Girl by Orrie Hitt; Beacon Book #B238, 1959.

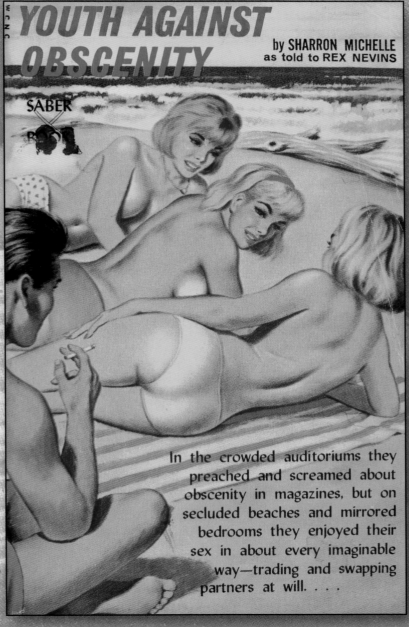

YOUTH AGAINST OBSCENITY

by SHARRON MICHELLE
as told to REX NEVINS

SABER

In the crowded auditoriums they preached and screamed about obscenity in magazines, but on secluded beaches and mirrored bedrooms they enjoyed their sex in about every imaginable way—trading and swapping partners at will. . . .

Love slow… Fight fast…
Drink more… Talk less…
Mountain women and mountain men
live that way, and that's the way they
want to live. There's no use trying to
make them talk more, because they
don't see the use of it. And there's no
use trying to make them drink less,
because mountain dew isn't made for
light drinking. By the same token, you
can't slow down a mountain man's
willingness to fight… or speed up a
mountain woman's surrender to love.

ORIGINAL
NOVELS

The Life and Loves of a Reckless Mountain Girl

SHANTY ROAD

by Whit Harrison

35¢
No. 742

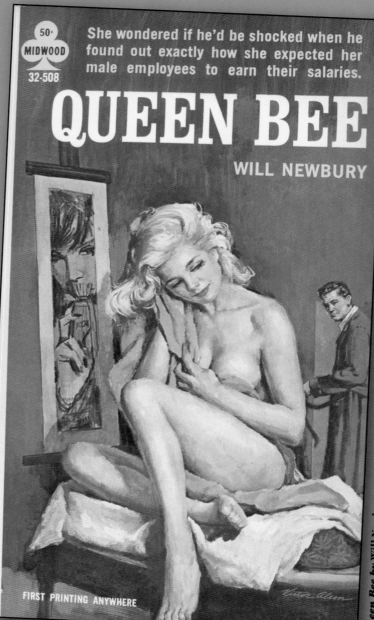

50¢
MIDWOOD
32-508

She wondered if he'd be shocked when he found out exactly how she expected her male employees to earn their salaries.

QUEEN BEE

WILL NEWBURY

FIRST PRINTING ANYWHERE

Queen Bee by Will Newbury; Midwood Book #32-508, 1963. Cover art by Victor Olson.

"Relax, darling," she murmured huskily, running her fingertips up his thigh. "As long as you want this account as badly as you say, I'm sure we'll be able to do business.

You give me what I want and I'll give you what you want."

Brian trembled under the tantalizing play of her knowing fingers and cleared his throat. "Very simple…" Lila leaned back and extended her long legs. "You can begin by taking off my stockings…"

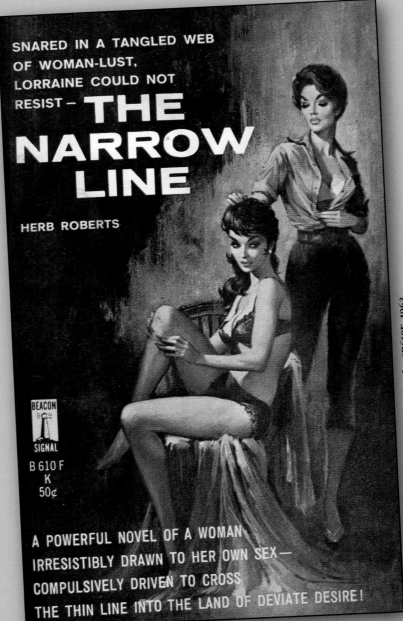

SNARED IN A TANGLED WEB
OF WOMAN-LUST,
LORRAINE COULD NOT
RESIST — **THE
NARROW
LINE**

HERB ROBERTS

BEACON
SIGNAL

B 610 F
K
50¢

A POWERFUL NOVEL OF A WOMAN
IRRESISTIBLY DRAWN TO HER OWN SEX —
COMPULSIVELY DRIVEN TO CROSS
THE THIN LINE INTO THE LAND OF DEVIATE DESIRE!

The Narrow Line by Herb Roberts; Beacon Books #B610F, 1963.

More Must-Have Guides
from Gary Lovisi

FREE

Bad Girls Wallpaper
&
Bad Girl
of the Week

Get yours today!

www.badgirlsneedlove2.com/enewsletter

Note: You must have a valid e-mail address to receive your free bad girls.